100 QUESTIONS about the HUMAN BODY

and all the answers too!

Written and Illustrated by
Simon Abbott

PETER PAUPER PRESS, INC.
White Plains, New York

PETER PAUPER PRESS

In 1928, at the age of twenty-two, Peter Beilenson began printing books on a small press in the basement of his parents' home in Larchmont, New York. Peter—and later, his wife, Edna—sought to create fine books that sold at "prices even a pauper could afford."

Today, still family owned and operated, Peter Pauper Press continues to honor our founders' legacy of quality, value, and fun for big kids and small kids alike.

Designed by Heather Zschock

Text and illustrations copyright © 2019 by Simon Abbott

Published by Peter Pauper Press, Inc.
202 Mamaroneck Avenue
White Plains, New York 10601 USA

Published in the United Kingdom and Europe by Peter Pauper Press, Inc.
c/o White Pebble International
Unit 2, Plot 11 Terminus Rd.
Chichester, West Sussex PO19 8TX, UK

Library of Congress Cataloging-in-Publication Data
Names: Abbott, Simon, 1967- author, illustrator.
Title: 100 questions about the human body : and all the answers too! / written and illustrated by Simon Abbott.
Other titles: One hundred questions about the human body
Description: White Plains, New York : Peter pauper Press, Inc., [2019] | Series: 100 questions | Audience: Age 7+
Identifiers: LCCN 2019006307 | ISBN 9781441331014 (hardcover : alk. paper)
Subjects: LCSH: Human physiology--Miscellanea--Juvenile literature. | Children's questions and answers.
Classification: LCC QP37 .A24 2019 | DDC 612.0076--dc23 LC record available at https://lccn.loc.gov/2019006307
ISBN 978-1-4413-3101-4
Manufactured for Peter Pauper Press, Inc.
Printed in Hong Kong

7 6 5 4 3 2 1

Visit us at www.peterpauper.com

WELCOME!

You've been living in your amazing body your whole life, but how well do you actually know it?

What's a cell?

Why do people fart?

How can you take good care of your body?

Your body is an incredible brain-boggling, heart-pumping, muscle-clenching machine.

Let's learn all about it and sniff out the facts from the fiction!

AMAZING ANATOMY

Your body is made of thousands of parts, all working hard to keep you alive!
Let's journey inside this sensational system to see what's going on.

What does anatomy mean?

It's a body's structure. The study of it dates
back to Ancient Egyptian experts, who identified
most major body parts over three thousand
years ago!

What is our body made of?

There are four major elements (basic building blocks of the universe) that make up
what we are, as shown in the chart below. These elements come together to make
everything in us, including water (which makes up about 60 percent of our bodies).
Zoom a bit further out, and these molecules come together to form our cells, which
are the basic biological building blocks for everything from our head to our toes.

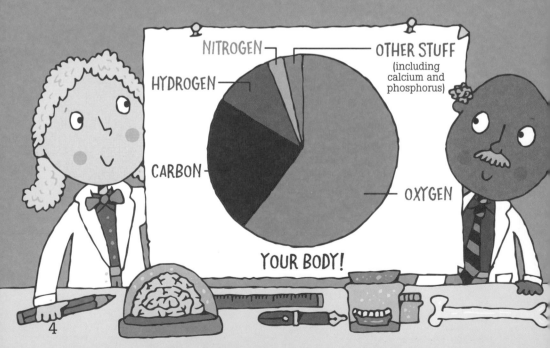

How are organs made?

Cells that are similar join together to make a tissue. Two or more tissues link up to form an organ. Take a look at 10 essential organs in the diagram.

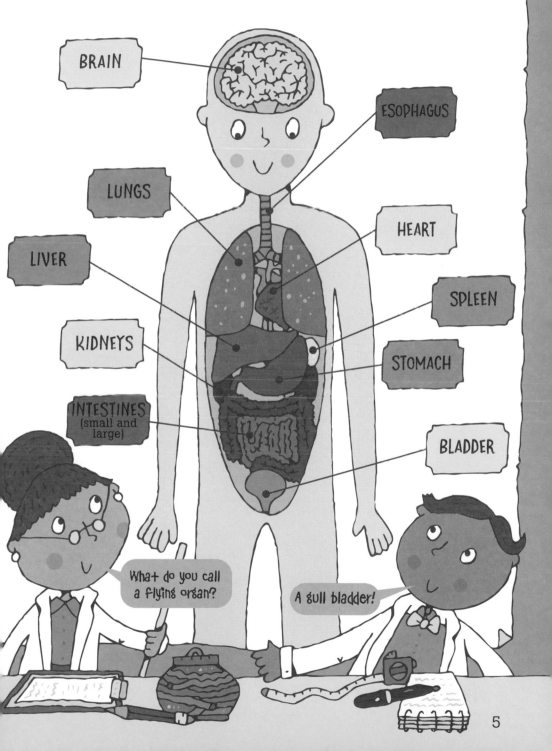

What systems do we have?

You're kept alive by your body systems. A system is created when two or more related organs are linked together. Just take a look!

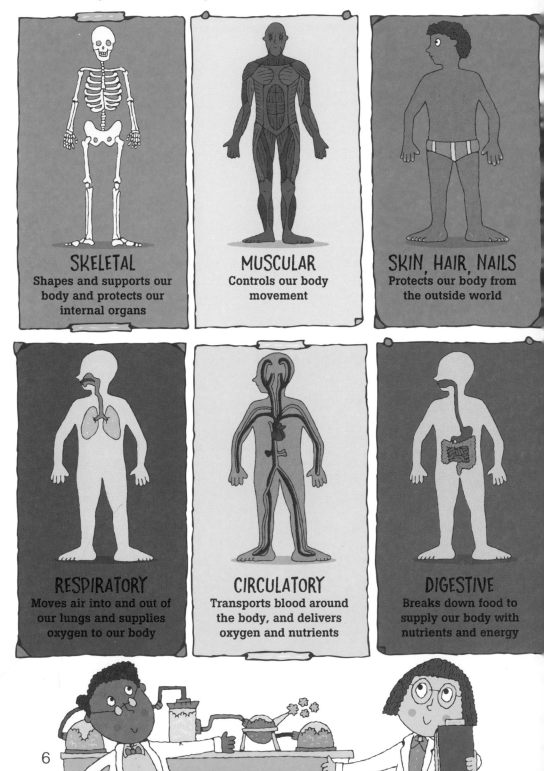

SKELETAL
Shapes and supports our body and protects our internal organs

MUSCULAR
Controls our body movement

SKIN, HAIR, NAILS
Protects our body from the outside world

RESPIRATORY
Moves air into and out of our lungs and supplies oxygen to our body

CIRCULATORY
Transports blood around the body, and delivers oxygen and nutrients

DIGESTIVE
Breaks down food to supply our body with nutrients and energy

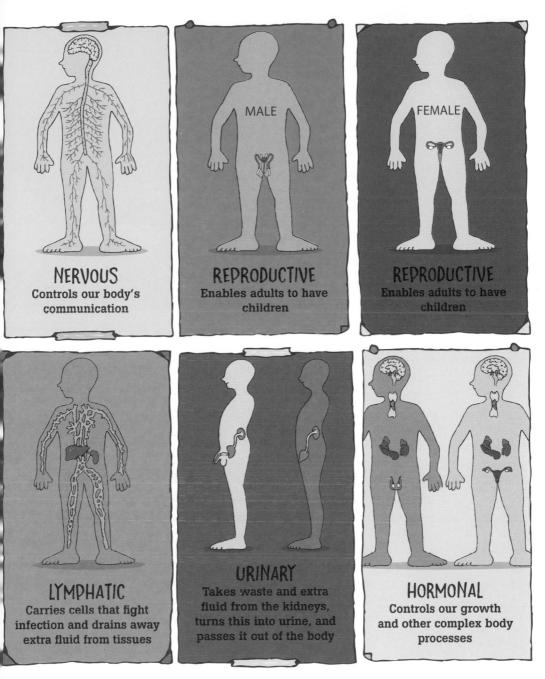

NERVOUS
Controls our body's communication

REPRODUCTIVE
Enables adults to have children

MALE

REPRODUCTIVE
Enables adults to have children

FEMALE

LYMPHATIC
Carries cells that fight infection and drains away extra fluid from tissues

URINARY
Takes waste and extra fluid from the kidneys, turns this into urine, and passes it out of the body

HORMONAL
Controls our growth and other complex body processes

Now close the book and see how many systems you can remember!

FACT or FICTION?

If we lose an organ are we ... how can I put this ... dead?
We can survive without an appendix, gallbladder, or spleen, and some people have only one kidney or lung. The small intestine can replace the stomach, and if some necessary organs, such as the liver or heart, stop working, transplant surgery can swap in a replacement.

LET'S CELEBRATE OUR CELLS!

Cells come in all shapes and sizes, joining together like building blocks to create you! Let's take a closer look at these microscopic miracles that make up every single part of your body.

How many cells does my body contain?
An average human is made of over 30 trillion cells. If you counted them at a rate of one per second, it could take over a million years!

Can I see them?
Only with a mega powerful microscope. Red blood cells, for instance, come in at a minuscule 0.00003 inches (0.0075 mm).

So, what do cells look like?

There are around 200 types of cells in your body. Let's get the low-down on the top five.

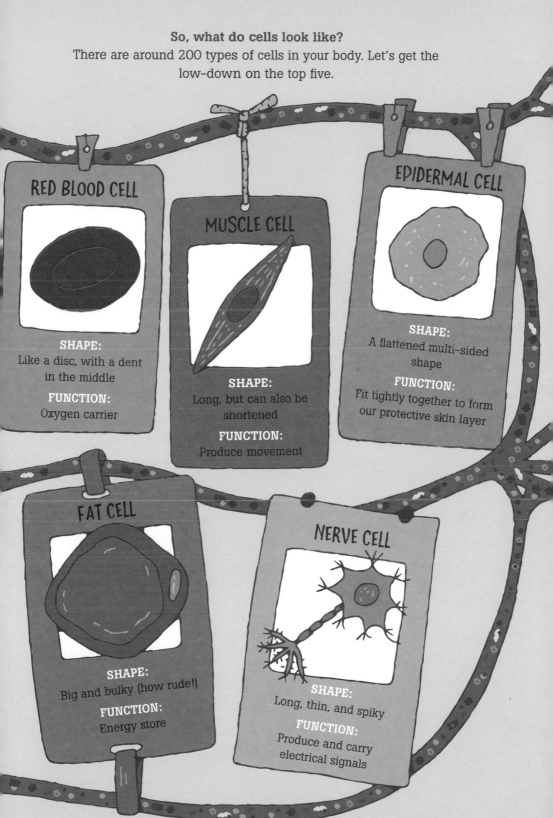

RED BLOOD CELL

SHAPE:
Like a disc, with a dent in the middle

FUNCTION:
Oxygen carrier

MUSCLE CELL

SHAPE:
Long, but can also be shortened

FUNCTION:
Produce movement

EPIDERMAL CELL

SHAPE:
A flattened multi-sided shape

FUNCTION:
Fit tightly together to form our protective skin layer

FAT CELL

SHAPE:
Big and bulky (how rude!)

FUNCTION:
Energy store

NERVE CELL

SHAPE:
Long, thin, and spiky

FUNCTION:
Produce and carry electrical signals

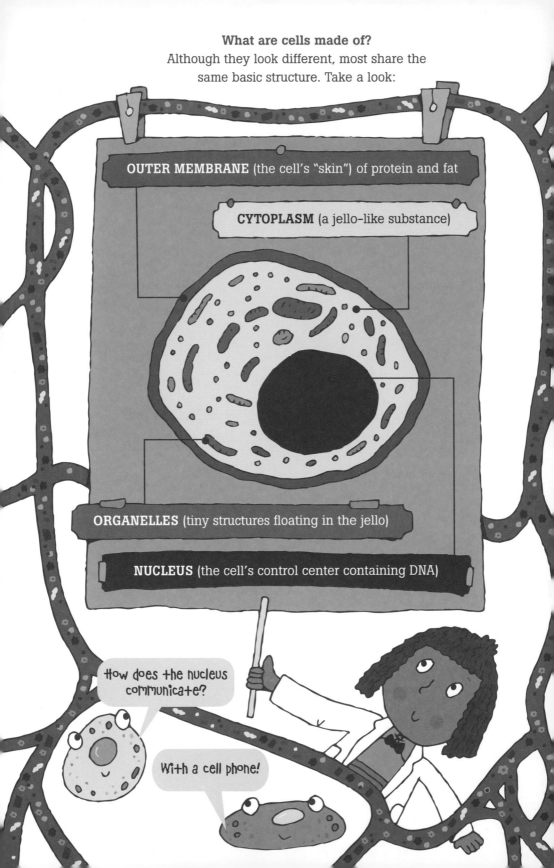

What are cells made of?
Although they look different, most share the
same basic structure. Take a look:

OUTER MEMBRANE (the cell's "skin") of protein and fat

CYTOPLASM (a jello-like substance)

ORGANELLES (tiny structures floating in the jello)

NUCLEUS (the cell's control center containing DNA)

How does the nucleus communicate?

With a cell phone!

DNA? What does that stand for?

It's short for (take a deep breath) deoxyribonucleic *(dee–AWK–si–RHY–boh–noo–clay–ik)* acid. It contains a unique set of codes controlling the cell's function and the incredible pattern for human life. These codes are different for every single person (apart from identical twins, whose DNA is exactly the same).

How does DNA determine the pattern for human life?

Sections of DNA, or genes, provide the body's manual for its entire life. Genes hold the instructions for your growth, survival, and reproduction. They're chemical codes that determine the color of your hair and eyes, your height, and your health and natural skills. We inherit our genes from our biological parents, which is why we might look like them.

Could we make an exact copy of ourselves from our own DNA?

Scientists have been experimenting with copying (or cloning) some animal species with very mixed results. In 1996, Scottish scientists cloned a sheep, Dolly. Dolly lived for only six years, which is far shorter than most sheep live. Today, scientists expect the cloned animal should be very similar to the original.

How long does a cell last?

The simple answer is that all cells have different life-spans. A colon cell lasts less than four days, skin cells hang around for around two weeks, and some brain-based nerve cells can survive your whole lifetime! Cells divide in two to replace the ones that are worn out in a process called mitosis.

NO BONES ABOUT IT

Imagine your body without its skeleton! You'd be a shapeless blob, trying to grip this amazing book! Let's bone up on this sensational structure.

How many bones are there in the human body?
206 bones! We're actually born with more—around 300—but some bones join together as we grow up.

How do our bones fit together?
Our bones meet each other at our joints, where they're attached to each other by tough cords called ligaments and to our muscles by cords called tendons. There are different types of joints, including ball-and-socket (which allows full circular motion, like where your shoulder meets your arm), saddle (which allows back-and-forth and side-to-side motion, like where your thumb meets your hand), and hinge (which only allows either back-and-forth or side-to-side but not both, like your knees).

BALL AND SOCKET   SADDLE   HINGE

If our skeleton is the solid support for our bodies, is this skeleton heavy?
No! Our bones are incredibly light and make up just 15 percent of a person's body mass. In an adult, that's about the same weight as a dachshund dog.

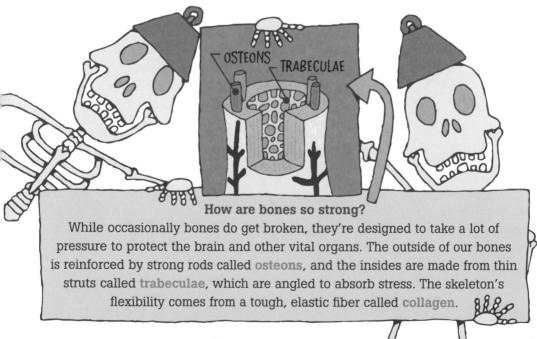

OSTEONS   TRABECULAE

How are bones so strong?
While occasionally bones do get broken, they're designed to take a lot of pressure to protect the brain and other vital organs. The outside of our bones is reinforced by strong rods called osteons, and the insides are made from thin struts called trabeculae, which are angled to absorb stress. The skeleton's flexibility comes from a tough, elastic fiber called collagen.

What goes on inside a bone? Are they just dry, hollow tubes?

No way! In certain bones you'll find marrow, a soft jello-like tissue. Red bone marrow is the body's blood factory, making over 200 billion new cells each day. Much of this turns to yellow bone marrow as you get older, and becomes a store for fat cells.

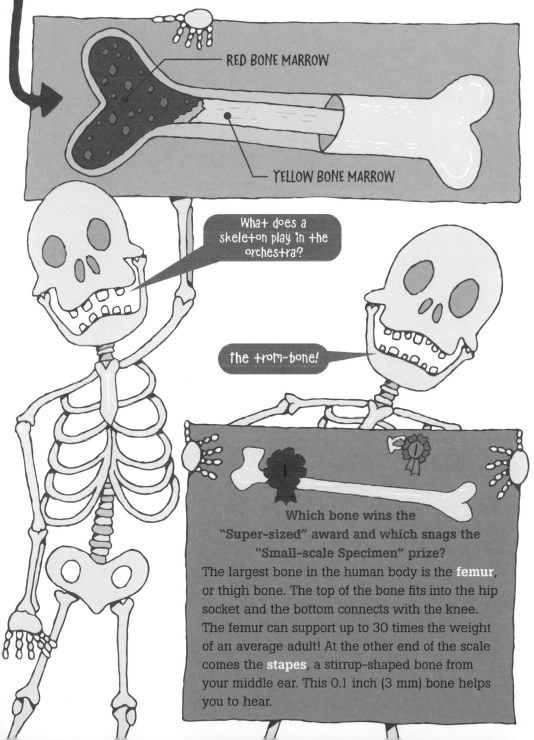

RED BONE MARROW

YELLOW BONE MARROW

What does a skeleton play in the orchestra?

the trom-bone!

Which bone wins the "Super-sized" award and which snags the "Small-scale Specimen" prize?

The largest bone in the human body is the femur, or thigh bone. The top of the bone fits into the hip socket and the bottom connects with the knee. The femur can support up to 30 times the weight of an average adult! At the other end of the scale comes the stapes, a stirrup-shaped bone from your middle ear. This 0.1 inch (3 mm) bone helps you to hear.

MUSCLE POWER!

We don't need to hit the gym to discover the importance of our muscular system. Our every movement is made possible by our hardworking muscles. Let's find out how!

What are muscles made from?
Muscle tissue is made up of long cells. Movements are controlled by nerve signals sent by your brain. The muscle then shortens (or contracts), pulling parts of your body into different positions.

MUSCLE CELL

SHORTENED OR CONTRACTED MUSCLE CELL

Can a muscle push as well as pull?
Nope. But to get around this, muscles are often arranged in pairs to perform opposite tasks. Let's take the arm for instance. When a message hits the **bicep**, it shortens and pulls the arm up, while the **tricep** relaxes on the other side. To pull the arm down, the tricep muscle contracts and the bicep chills out. Job done!

BICEP CONTRACTED

TRICEP RELAXED

BICEP RELAXED

TRICEP CONTRACTED

What has two legs but cannot walk?

Pants!

Are there different sorts of muscles?
There are three types of muscles in our body. Take a look!

MUSCLE

FUNCTION

Skeletal Muscle

These muscles move our bones. We decide to move them, so they are called voluntary muscles. There are over 640 skeletal muscles. The cells of these muscles are often called fibers.

Smooth Muscle

These muscles are packed together in layers and line the airway, digestive system, and bladder. They work automatically to keep important body functions going.

Cardiac Muscle

This muscle contracts all through your life to keep the heart beating. Unlike skeletal muscles, it never takes a break. Hooray!

What happens to my muscles when I exercise?
Your whole body helps out when you play sports or exercise. Your heart beats faster to pump more blood to your muscles and give them the oxygen and nutrients they need to complete the task. By contrast, your digestive system slows down to save the energy that your muscles need.

UNDER YOUR SKIN!

It's our body's biggest organ and our very own central heating system. Time to investigate the skin that we're in!

What's so great about our skin?

Skin is our protective waterproof coat, defending our body from infection and the weather. It lets us have the sense of touch and keeps our temperature just right!

The outer layer that you can see, the epidermis, acts like a built-in coat that germs, dirt, and ultraviolet light can't pass through.

What happens beneath the top layer?

Underneath the epidermis is the dermis. Here you'll find nerves, blood vessels, nails, and hair follicles. It also helps control our body temperatures. If you're hot, blood vessels in the dermis widen. This increases the blood flow to the skin, which takes heat away from your body. When you're cold, blood vessels narrow, decreasing the blood flow to your skin.

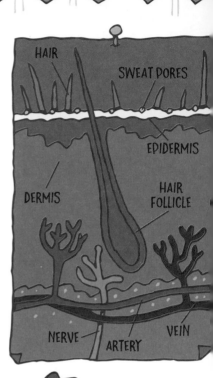

HAIR
SWEAT PORES
EPIDERMIS
HAIR FOLLICLE
DERMIS
NERVE
ARTERY
VEIN

Phew! Are there any other ways to cool down?

Sweat it out! Our millions of sweat glands release fluid (99% water) onto the skin's surface when you're boiling hot. This sweat evaporates, taking heat away from your body and cooling you down. Chill!

If it's our body's biggest organ, then how big is this layer of skin?
The average adult's skin weighs about 8 pounds (3.6 kg), and rolled out flat takes up an area of 22 square feet (2 square meters). It can be as thin as 0.02 inches (0.5 mm) on your eyelids, or as thick as 0.16 inches (4 mm) on the soles of your feet.

Why do we get goose bumps?
In cold temperatures, tiny muscles attached to each hair contract, causing the hair to stand upright and trap warm air. That was great when we had a thick fur coat, but it's not so useful now! Maybe you get goose bumps when you're watching a scary movie, or when you're a little emotional after a great sports game. This is caused by the release of a chemical called adrenaline which, among other things, causes skin muscles to contract.

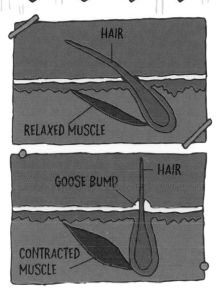

HAIR

RELAXED MUSCLE

GOOSE BUMP — HAIR

CONTRACTED MUSCLE

My friends and I all have different skin colors. Why is that?
It's all down to a pigment that your body produces called melanin. A person with darker skin has large amounts of melanin, and a person with lighter skin has a small amount. Simple!

Why do some people have freckles?
Freckles happen when melanin-making cells make even more melanin thanks to a healthy dose of sunlight.

What else helps to shield our bodies from the outside?

Nails protect the ends of our toes and fingers. These are made from dead skin cells strengthened by a protein called keratin. A typical fingernail grows 0.12 inches (3 mm) per month, as new cells growing at the root push the nail forward. They grow much faster in the summer months, so keep those nail clippers handy on the beach!

Does our hair offer any protection?

It sure does! It keeps us warm by trapping heat, and protects the scalp from the hot sun. Our eyelashes and eyebrows keep sweat and debris out of our eyes. Hairs in our nostrils and ear canals keep out dust, grime, and even insects. Our nose hair also helps control the temperature of the air we breathe in.

What is our hair made of?

Hair is really just long strands of keratin, the same protein in your nails. Hairs grow from tiny openings called follicles in the dermis skin layer, at a rate of 0.5 inches (1.25 cm) per month. The hair growing inside the follicle is alive, while the hair shaft itself is considered dead.

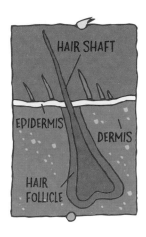

Why do humans have so many different hair colors?

Melanin inside the follicle determines whether we have blond, black, red, or brown hair. As we get older, our follicles make less and less melanin, so our hair loses its color and becomes transparent. This is why older folks look like they have silver or gray hair.

How many hairs do we have on our head?

Humans have an average of 100,000 hairs on our heads. But hair isn't just found on our heads—we have about 5 million follicles all over our bodies.

WONDERS OF THE WORLD

Let's have a roll call of anatomical award winners! These human high-achievers will be tough to defeat. Are you up for a challenge?

Which super-human is the tallest on record?
That prize goes to Robert Wadlow, who reached a dizzying height of 8 ft, 11 in (2.75 m) in 1940. To be fair, that's only half the height of a giraffe!

Who wins the tiniest trophy?
Chandra Bahadur Dangi measured 21.5 in (54.6 cm) high. That's just half the height of a baseball bat!

Who grew the longest fingernails?
Shridhar Chillal from India.
He started growing his nails at 14 years old,
and 66 years later they had a combined
length of 29 ft, 10.1 in (909.6 cm).

Whose hair is head and shoulders above the rest?

The longest documented hair was grown by Xie Qiuping of China, whose locks measure 18 ft, 5.54 in (5.627 m). That's three times longer than your bed!

While we're talking hair, which beard grower gets the first-place prize?

"King of the Whiskers" is Hans Nilsen Langseth from Norway. At his funeral in 1927, his beard, which measured a whopping 17 ft, 6 in (5.36 m), was lopped off at his final request, so it could be saved for future generations.

Who's "King of the Popsicle" with the world's longest tongue?

American Nick Stoeberl has everyone licked with his 3.98 in (10.1 cm) tongue. The female record for the widest tongue is held by Emily Schlenker at 2.89 in (7.33 cm) at its widest point. The first-placed male is Emily's dad, Byron, with a tongue-tastic 3.37 in (8.57 cm) wide.

EVERY BREATH YOU TAKE

Every single cell in your body needs a constant supply of oxygen, which we get from the air around us. Let's get the low-down on our indispensable air-supply!

How do we get oxygen into our body?

We automatically breathe in through our mouth and nose about 20,000 times a day, gulping down about 388 cu ft (11,000 liters) of air throughout that time. A strong tube of muscle called a **trachea** carries this air to our lungs. Breathing in and out is controlled by a dome-shaped muscle called the **diaphragm**.

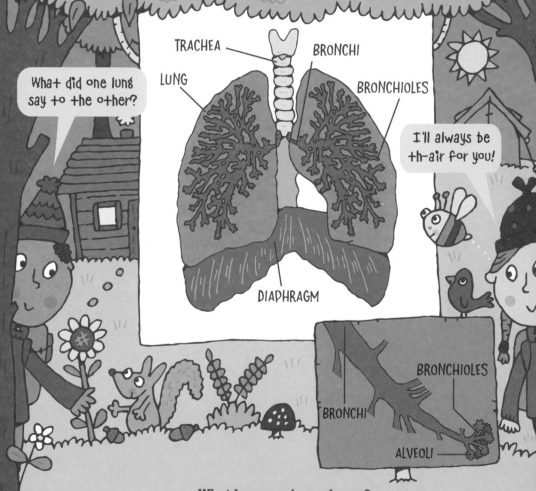

TRACHEA
BRONCHI
LUNG
BRONCHIOLES
DIAPHRAGM
BRONCHIOLES
BRONCHI
ALVEOLI

What did one lung say to the other?

I'll always be th-air for you!

What happens in my lungs?

Think of the inside of your lungs as an upside-down tree. The trachea "trunk" divides into two tubes called **bronchi**. One of these tubes leads to the left lung, the other to the right. The bronchi then split into smaller branches called **bronchioles**, which are narrower than hairs. At the end of each bronchiole are tiny air sacs called **alveoli**.

What do these air sacs do?

They may be mini, but the 400 million plus alveoli in our lungs are an essential part of our breathing. The walls of the alveoli are very thin, so they can easily release oxygen into our bloodstream. They also let a gas called **carbon dioxide** back into our airway, which is removed from our bodies as we breathe out. This is called **gas exchange**.

ALVEOLI

DEOXYGENATED BLOOD IN

CARBON DIOXIDE OUT

OXYGEN IN

OXYGENATED BLOOD OUT

RED BLOOD CELLS

GAS EXCHANGE

CARBON DIOXIDE

Why does our body need to remove carbon dioxide when it breathes out?

Carbon dioxide, which comes from our cells as they make energy, dissolves into our **blood plasma**. This can be toxic if there's too much of it. To prevent this, our body gets rid of excess carbon dioxide by breathing it out.

FINGER ON THE PULSE!

During an average lifetime your hard-working heart will pump 800 million pints (379 million liters) of blood around your body. It's time to get the bottom line on this brilliant blood transport network. Read on!

Does our blood transport network have a name?
Sure! It's the cardiovascular system. It delivers oxygen and nutrients to our cells, and carries away any waste products, too. In just one day, your blood travels an incredible 12,000 miles (19,000 km) through tubes called arteries, veins, and capillaries.

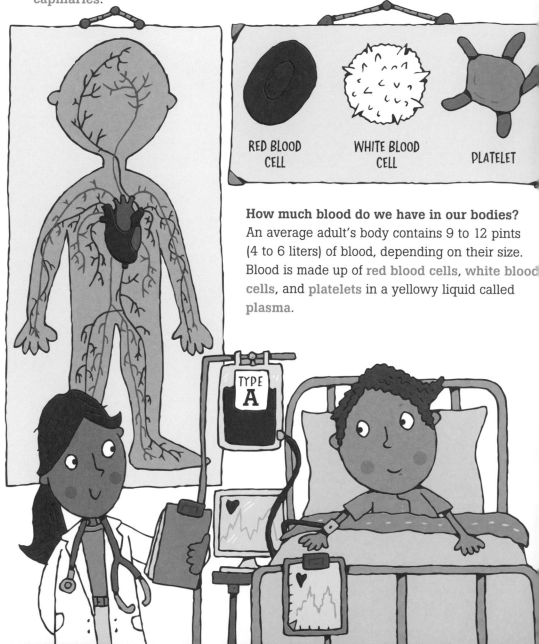

RED BLOOD
CELL

WHITE BLOOD
CELL

PLATELET

How much blood do we have in our bodies?
An average adult's body contains 9 to 12 pints (4 to 6 liters) of blood, depending on their size. Blood is made up of red blood cells, white blood cells, and platelets in a yellowy liquid called plasma.

TYPE
A

What different jobs do the blood cells have?

The most common are red blood cells. They contain a red protein called hemoglobin *(HEE-moh-gloh-bin)*, which allows the cells to transport and release oxygen around the body. Just 1 percent of your blood is made of white blood cells, which protect the body from invasion. They track down and digest disease-causing germs, and some discharge antibodies that fight infection. Platelets are the clever cells that seal cuts and scratches by forming blood clots.

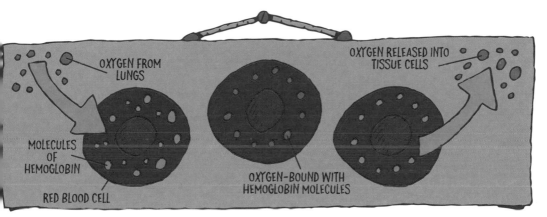

OXYGEN FROM LUNGS

OXYGEN RELEASED INTO TISSUE CELLS

MOLECULES OF HEMOGLOBIN

OXYGEN-BOUND WITH HEMOGLOBIN MOLECULES

RED BLOOD CELL

What are blood groups?

In the 1900s, scientist Karl Landsteiner discovered that most people belong to four different blood types: A, O, B, and AB. If you were in an accident and needed a blood transfusion, you'd get blood that matches your own type to keep your body from rejecting the wrong type of blood. (A blood transfusion is what doctors do when a person has lost a lot of blood. They take blood that a healthy person has donated and put it in the body of the person who lost it.)

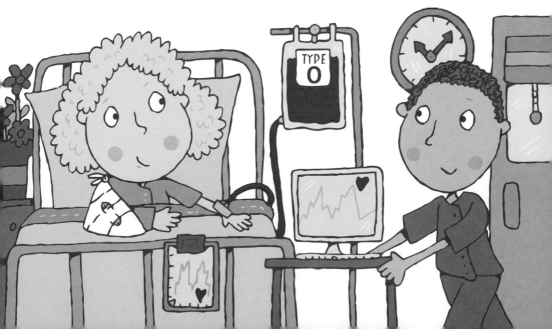

TYPE O

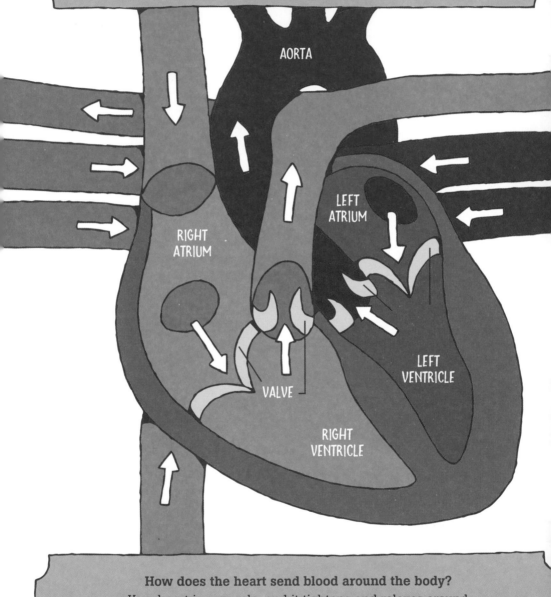

The engine room of our blood transport network is the heart. How big is this control center of our cardiovascular system? It's about the size of a clenched fist, and an adult heart is as heavy as a hamster.

AORTA

RIGHT ATRIUM

LEFT ATRIUM

VALVE

LEFT VENTRICLE

RIGHT VENTRICLE

How does the heart send blood around the body? Your heart is a muscle, and it tightens and relaxes around 70 times a minute to pump blood out through your arteries and back to the heart through your veins.

What goes on inside the heart?

The heart is split into two halves, and is separated by a wall of muscle called the septum. The right side of the heart is smaller and less powerful. It receives oxygen-poor blood from the body, then sends this to the lungs. The larger left side of the heart receives oxygen-rich blood from the lungs, which it then pumps out around the body.

Why did the nurse have a red pen?

In case she needed to draw blood!

What is a heartbeat?

The heart contains valves which control the blood circulation's one-way system (otherwise it could get quite confusing in there!). Every time a valve closes it causes a "lub dub" thumping noise. This is a heartbeat!

VALVE OPENS.
BLOOD CAN FLOW THROUGH.

VALVE CLOSES.
BLOOD CANNOT FLOW BACKWARD.

Why do doctors and nurses check a patient's pulse?

As blood rushes through your arteries it makes them bulge, which creates a pulse, or regular beat that can be felt on the wrist or neck. This is checked to see how quickly your blood is pumping through your body. A change to a patient's heart rate, or a weak pulse, may mean that there is a medical problem that needs attention.

FEAST ON THE FACTS!

It may start with a bite-sized snack, but it's got a day-long journey ahead through your digestive system. Now open wide and devour data about digestion!

Where does the digestive journey begin?
The first stop is your mouth. Let's see what's going on!

TONGUE
Keeps food in place when chewing
Essential for speech

BACK OF THE TONGUE
Stops microbes from entering the body

LIPS
Holds food in your mouth

TEETH
Molars grind food
Incisors cut food
Canines tear food

SALIVARY GLANDS
Produce saliva, a liquid that softens food and lets it slide down the throat easily

SOFT PALATE
Stops food from getting into your nose

UVULA
Helps with speech and swallowing

EPIGLOTTIS
Stops food from entering the airway

How many teeth do we have?

We start out with 20 "baby" (or "milk") teeth which begin growing when we are half a year old. From the age of six, we start to grow our 32 adult teeth (16 at the top, 16 at the bottom), replacing the baby teeth that become loose and fall out as our jaws grow.

What helps us taste our food?

Our tongue is covered in taste buds, which are nerve endings. This tells us whether a mouthful is sweet, salty, sour, or bitter, and senses the temperature and texture of our food.

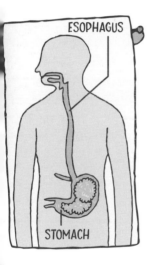

We've tasted and chewed our food, then covered it with saliva. What's next?

It slides down a long food pipe called the esophagus and into the stomach. As soon as it arrives, the stomach muscles begin to churn the food, and acid is released to break it down even further.

Stomach acid is super-strong and can eat through skin, bone, and almost anything you swallow. Don't put it to the test though!

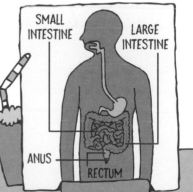

Where's the next stop on our digestive adventure after the stomach?

Your food is now a thick, dark, mushy substance and has arrived at your 20-foot (6 m) long small intestine. Here, your body removes 90 percent of the food's nutrients and transfers them to your blood through tiny 0.04 in (1 mm) structures called villi. The remaining undigested food components are squeezed through to the large intestine, then squished into a short tube called the rectum. Finally, a double ring of muscles called the anus pushes out your food waste as poop!

Why is poop brown?

It's all due to an orange-yellow pigment called **bilirubin**, which comes from dead red blood cells. However, you can change the color of your poop by eating certain foods like licorice, beets, and blueberries.

How much poop do we produce?

An average adult ejects around 15 ounces (425 g) per day. We're looking at around 25,000 pounds (11,340 kg) in a lifetime, which is the equivalent to three hippos!

What does healthy poop look like?

If you're healthy, well, and eating your greens, it should be soft and shaped like a sausage. If it's a brown, soupy liquid, you may have **diarrhea**. That's just your body's way of getting rid of the contents of your digestive system as quickly as possible, because you're sick or you ate something that might harm you.

Why do we barf?

There's one similar reason: Your body vomits because it detects a bad bacteria or virus and needs to press the "eject all contents" button! Other reasons to throw up include motion sickness (when you feel sick because you're moving a lot), stress, or eating too much or too quickly, so take care of yourself!

Why does vomit smell like cheese?

When your good stomach bacteria break down food, **butyric acid**, which has a strong smell, is created. This is the same process that takes place when cheese is fermented. (Have you eaten, by the way?)

Why am I such a farty-pants?

Everyone passes gas around 14 times a day. Sometimes you eat too fast without chewing properly. Large chunks of food are hard to digest, and you've probably gulped down large amounts of air as you're eating, resulting in a build-up. Another reason is that as good bacteria process your food, they produce a whiffy gas blend of **hydrogen sulfide**, **carbon dioxide**, and **methane**.

Excuse me! Why do I burp?

You swallow air when you eat or drink, and this can get trapped in your stomach. Fizzy drinks contain gas bubbles and, again, this builds up in your tummy. The gas makes its escape back up your throat and reappears as a booming burp!

MYTH BUSTERS

Let's sort the cast-iron facts and the far-fetched fiction behind the human body. Time to dig out the toe-tingling truth!

Is it true that if all the body's blood vessels were spread out, they would be long enough to stretch around the Earth?
If you laid all your arteries, veins, and capillaries end to end, the total length would be 60,000 miles (96,560 km). That's two and a half times around the world!

Are a quarter of all your bones in your feet?
Do you remember how many bones we have in total? That's right—206! Well, there are 26 bones in each foot, making 52 in total. That's just over a quarter, so it's true!

Is it okay to wake a sleepwalker?
Sometimes! Sleepwalking happens when the brain makes a person get up and do things they'd normally do when they're awake. It's never a good idea to shake a sleepwalker awake, because they might fight back. Instead, guide a sleepwalker back to bed by nudging them in the right direction. If they're in danger, though, stand back and shout to startle them awake!

Do you really have to wait a half hour to swim if you've just eaten?
Nope! Eating before swimming won't channel all your blood to your digestive system, and you won't get tired and drown, which means swimming after eating is safe. You might get a stomach cramp from working too hard, but if you relax and stretch, you'll be back to doing the backstroke in no time!

GETTING ON YOUR NERVES!

Our unbelievable nervous system allows us to see, hear, feel, move, think, and remember. Let's link up with this system and make some astonishing discoveries.

What is our nervous system? It's a structure for control and communication, made of your nerves and brain. It is divided into the **central nervous system** (brain and spinal cord) and **peripheral nervous system** (nerves that branch out to the rest of the body).

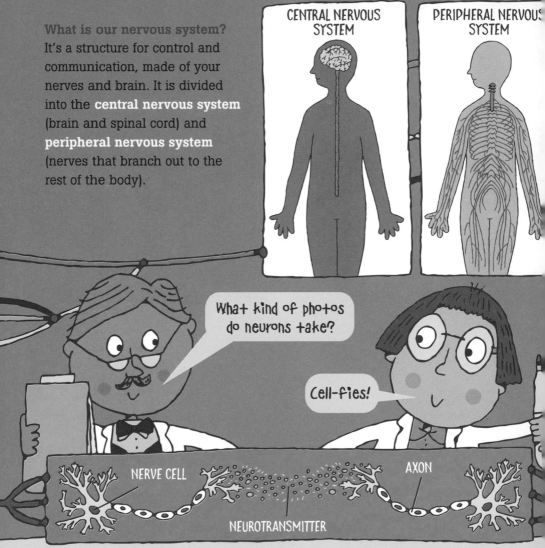

How do my nerves communicate?

Nerves carry messages between the brain and every organ and muscle, 24 hours a day. They send the brain a constant stream of data about what is going on inside and outside your body. When a neuron, or nerve cell, fires up, it emits a burst of electricity that flies down the axon (or the nerve's tail). Once this burst hits the end, it makes the axon release neurotransmitters, or tiny packets of chemicals that carry the nerve's message to the next cell.

Are there different types of nerves, just like there are different types of skin and muscle cells?

There are three main groups. **Motor nerves** carry messages from the brain to control our muscles. **Sensory nerves** react to light, sound, and touch. Sensory and motor neurons are connected by **association neurons**.

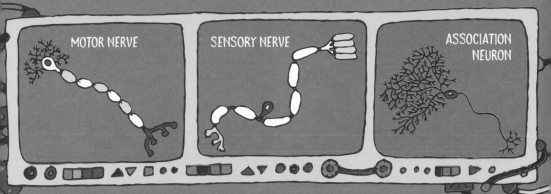

MOTOR NERVE

SENSORY NERVE

ASSOCIATION NEURON

What happens to our nervous system when we sleep?
Your brain just keeps on working! It's busy storing and sorting the information of the day, filing it away, and creating new memories. When we're asleep, we relax, and our brain uses the overall "downtime" to do a little housekeeping (by washing away toxins).

What are our senses?

We have five senses that enable us to experience the world around us: hearing, touch, sight, smell, and taste.

How do we hear?

Sound waves enter the ear canal and beat against the eardrum to make it vibrate. This makes your ear bones (or ossicles) move, with the stirrup pushing and pulling at the entrance to the inner ear (or cochlea). Sound-detecting hair cells sense these movements and turn them into signals sent to the brain.

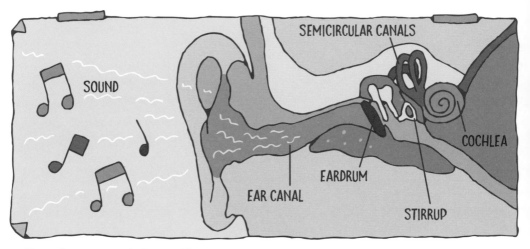

How do we stay balanced?

Our inner ear contains three fluid-filled tubes called semicircular canals. As we move our heads, fluids in these canals slosh around, helping our heads detect direction. This system works with our eyes, skin sensors, and stretch sensors to help our brains adjust and stop us from falling over.

How do we see?

The lens in each eye focuses light rays through the pupil, the hole in the front of our eye, onto the back of our eyeball, or retina. Here, receptors record the light, shadow, and color of an object, then send this information along the optic nerve to the brain.

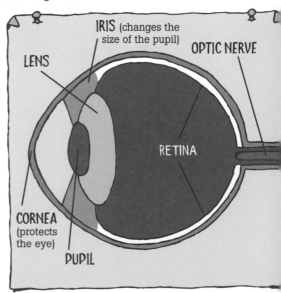

How do we feel?

Touch receptors in our skin register temperature and pressure—and three million of them detect pain. When we touch or feel anything, the pressure on our skin makes the receptors move. This triggers a message to the brain which figures out whether the signal means pain, heat, cold, light pressure, or deep pressure.

How do I smell?

Terrible! Only joking! As we inhale, odor molecules are sucked into the nose, where they are dissolved in mucus. (That's snot to you and me!) This mixture attaches itself to the tiny hairs that line your nasal cavity called cilia, which are attached to receptor cells. The odor molecule makes a signal which travels to the brain. Your body has around 12 million smell (or olfactory) receptors, which can sniff out around 10,000 different odors!

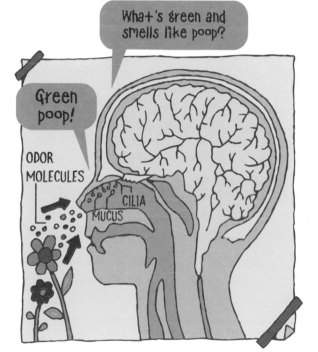

What's green and smells like poop?

Green poop!

ODOR MOLECULES

CILIA

MUCUS

Why can't I taste anything when I have a stuffy nose?

When you think of a food's flavor, what you're actually thinking of is a bunch of senses working together, namely taste, touch, and smell. When you bite into something, your taste gets a general sense (sweet, sour, salty, bitter, or savory), but nerves at the end of your nasal passage pick up on your snack's scent. These two pieces combine to tell you what you're eating. So if your sense of smell isn't working because of a stuffy nose, you're only getting half of the picture!

What is the brain made of?

The brain is 75 percent water and is the fattiest organ in the body. It's also made of two types of matter: gray (made up mostly of neurons) and white (made up mostly of coated axons, or nerve fibers). White matter transmits signals from the body to the gray matter, which processes information.

FACT OR FICTION?

Could you describe it as a pretty powerful computer?
I'll say! This 3-pound (1.36 kg) nerve center can perform a thousand trillion calculations per second!

How does the brain work?

Overall, the left side of the brain controls the right side of the body, and the right side of the brain controls the left side of the body. Beyond that, the brain is divided into several parts, or lobes:

LOBE:	CONTROLS:
Frontal Lobe	Personality, emotion, behavior, judgment, speech, movement
Parietal Lobe	Ability to read and write, sense of touch, special perception. Also interprets visual, hearing, and memory signals.
Occipital Lobe	Sight
Cerebellum	Balance, coordination, muscle movement
Brain Stem	Basic life functions, including heart rate, breathing, digestion, sleep, etc. Also relays messages from the spine to the rest of the brain.
Temporal Lobe	Memory, hearing, organization, the ability to understand language

How is the brain protected?

Your brain is a complicated but fragile machine. The cranial bones of your skull are the main things keeping it safe. There is a soft cushion of **membranes**, or **meninges**, and liquid called **cerebrospinal fluid** between the brain and the skull. Finally, the whole thing is topped off with your skin and hair as added security.

MENINGES SKULL

CEREBROSPINAL FLUID

How much memory can my brain store?

Scientists estimate that a human brain can hold around a million gigabytes, which is enough to store three million hours of TV shows! Look at the incredible amount of data the brain has on board:

Sensory Memory	Records sight, touch, and sound. Some of these memories only last a split second.
Short-term Memory	Stores information for a limited amount of time, sometimes only seconds.
Procedural Memory	Remembers skills like walking or riding a bike.
Episodic Memory	This recalls events in your life, such as a favorite vacation or first day of school.
Semantic Memory	Stores all the knowledge you collect, including the things you've read about in this book!

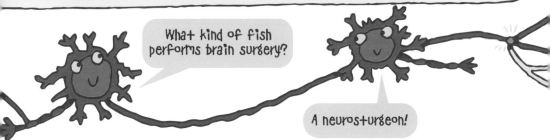

What kind of fish performs brain surgery?

A neurosturgeon!

What happens when the brain gets injured?

The brain may start sending out the wrong signals, or no signals at all. A patient may have trouble walking, talking, seeing, or hearing. Their personality could change, and they might even start talking in a foreign accent or language.

THE GREAT DEFENDER

Our body is under daily attack from viruses and bacteria. Let's see how we resist these microscopic invaders.

What are bacteria?

They are simple one-cell life-forms that can copy themselves quickly. Some bacteria are useful and hang around in our gut to help digestion. Others can cause serious illness by releasing poisons, called toxins.

What are viruses?

Viruses, tiny packets of DNA or RNA (a one-stranded cousin of DNA), hijack healthy cells and turn them into a laboratory where more viruses are formed. These are released into our body to infect more cells. As a group, viruses and bacteria that cause disease are called pathogens.

How does our body fight back?

Our first line of defense is the skin, which acts as a barrier against infection. We produce salty tears that wash away eye pathogens, and our nose traps germs with its sticky snot. Saliva contains chemicals that kill mouth bacteria, and earwax guards against invaders. Our stomach acid destroys the germs in our food. If all this fails, our body's internal immune system takes over.

What does our immune system do?

The system is managed by our white blood cells. These cells charge through our bloodstream, tracking down and killing bacteria and viruses. Antibodies, chemical proteins, attach themselves to invaders; these alert the white blood cells, which then surround and destroy the identified germ.

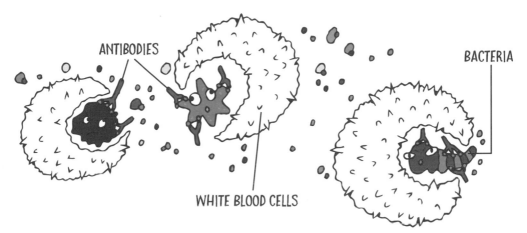

What is an allergy?

Sometimes our immune system gets it wrong and believes a harmless substance is attacking the body. This overreaction is called an allergy, and is often caused by animal hair, nuts, shellfish, or pollen.

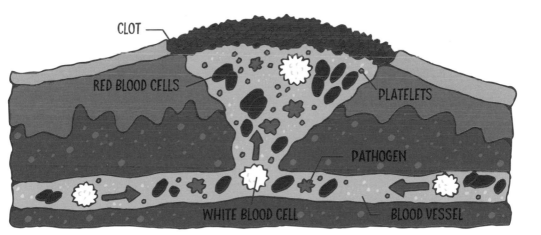

How does our body react when we get a cut?

When our skin is broken, our body's defense team leaps into action. First, blood vessels narrow, and platelets release a fiber that clots and seals the wound. Our blood vessels then widen, and the damaged tissue releases a chemical which triggers the white blood cells to seek and destroy pathogens. The site can now be handed over to the skin and tissue unit, which starts to fix the damage.

THE CLEAN-UP CREW

You're jam-packed with waste products that need collecting and ejecting! How does the body keep itself tidy?

What waste products does our body create?
Our cells continually release waste into the bloodstream. Our two hardworking **kidneys** filter and clean 2 pints (1.2 liters) of blood every single minute, removing the toxins and excess water, which become **urine**. This leaves you with around 3 pints (1.5 liters) of pee per day to dispose of.

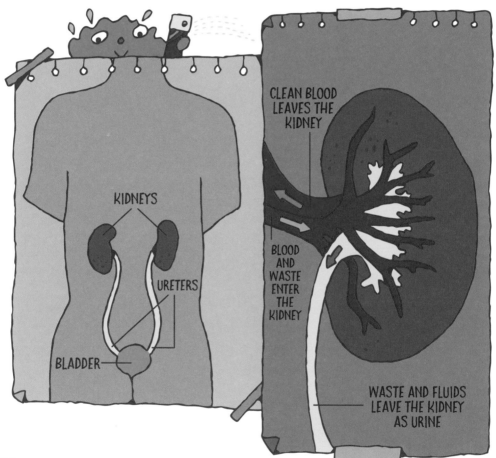

KIDNEYS

URETERS

BLADDER

CLEAN BLOOD LEAVES THE KIDNEY

BLOOD AND WASTE ENTER THE KIDNEY

WASTE AND FLUIDS LEAVE THE KIDNEY AS URINE

What happens to this urine?
Your pee travels in a one-way flow from the kidneys through the **ureter**, to the bladder. When the **bladder** fills up and stretches, pressure sensors send a signal to the brain. The ring of muscle that seals the bladder (the **sphincter**) then relaxes, allowing the urine to leave the body through a tube called the **urethra**.

What does our liver do?

Our biggest internal organ is a clean-up crusader! This 3 lb (1.3 kg) structure is the body's chemical processing center. As blood travels through the liver, it leaves behind unwelcome toxins. The liver produces a bitter green-yellow liquid, called bile, which is stored and concentrated in our gallbladder. The liquid bile gathers up the toxic waste and transfers it to the intestines to be pooped away!

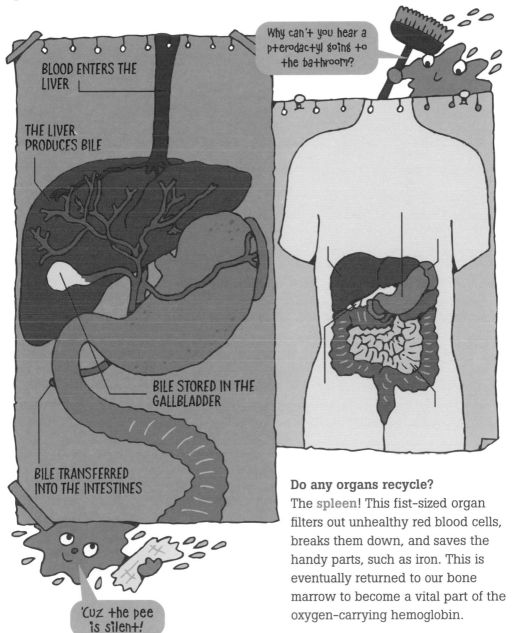

Do any organs recycle?

The spleen! This fist-sized organ filters out unhealthy red blood cells, breaks them down, and saves the handy parts, such as iron. This is eventually returned to our bone marrow to become a vital part of the oxygen-carrying hemoglobin.

THE BODY'S SECRET SIGNALS

If you thought that the nervous system had sole control over the body's messaging service, think again!

How does the body's second messaging service work?
It's called the **endocrine**, or **hormonal**, **system**. The glands in our body release chemical messages, which the blood delivers to cells and tissues with particular instructions. These messages are called **hormones**.

What do these glands control?
Glands are located in different parts of the body and produce hormones that have specific targets. Take a look!

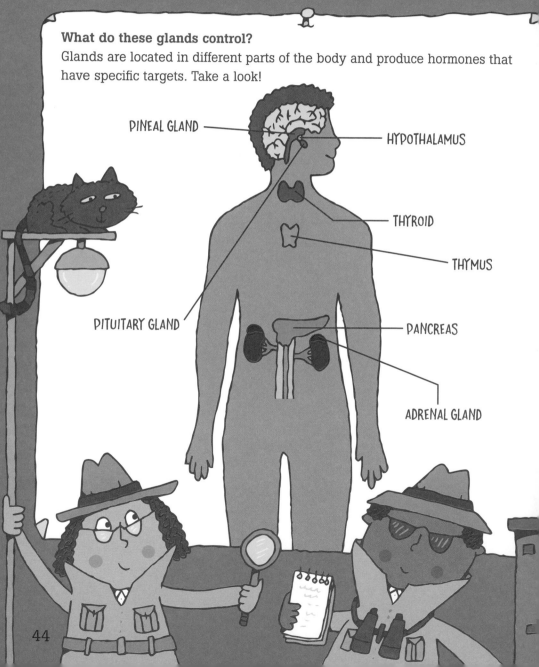

PINEAL GLAND

HYPOTHALAMUS

THYROID

THYMUS

PITUITARY GLAND

PANCREAS

ADRENAL GLAND

What functions do the glands in our body perform?

PINEAL GLAND	Controls sleep
HYPOTHALAMUS	Manages body temperature, appetite, and emotion
THYROID	Helps with bone and cell development and energy production
THYMUS	Helps protect the body against viruses and infections. This gland shrinks as you get older.
PITUITARY GLAND	Controls growth, hormone production in other glands, and our body's water levels
PANCREAS	Releases insulin and glucagon, which tops up our energy supply and helps break down food
ADRENAL GLAND	Makes hormones that keeps the body in balance while under stress

Now close the book and see if you can remember them all!

FACT OR FICTION?

Is the endocrine system the same for everyone?
Almost! Different glands in females and males produce hormones
that make their bodies mature as they grow to become adults.
Their bodies also change, but in different ways, to enable them
to have children when they're older.

SUPERHUMAN SUPERSTARS

Our body is a complex construction that lets us operate in astounding ways.
Take a look at the magnificent humans that drive their bodies to the max!

Who's the boss of temperature control?

Chilled-out Dutch adventurer Wim Hof is nicknamed, "The Iceman" for good
reason. He ran an arctic marathon shirtless, climbed to the frigid top of
Mt. Everest (the tallest mountain in the world) in shorts, and bathed in
freezing ice for a teeth-chattering 1 hour and 44 minutes. Brrrrrr!

What's the record for holding your breath?

Most untrained folks can hold their breath for around 30 seconds before
gulping for air. Aleix Segura Vendrell's record will take some deep breaths
to beat. This free diver managed a jaw-dropping 24 minutes and
3.45 seconds. Don't try that in the bathtub!

Who is the champ when it comes to staring contests?
At a competition in Australia, the final goggle-eyed contestants standing were Fergal "Eyesore" Fleming and Steven "Stare Master" Stagg. After an extraordinary 40 minutes and 59 seconds, Stagg finally blinked, leaving Fleming as the champ.

Who gets the Sensational Strength award?
Omar Hanapiev pulled a 635-ton tanker with his teeth! Let's hope the anchor was up!

Which super-speedy athlete has zoomed through the fastest mile?
Moroccan Hicham El Guerrouj holds the current world record, completing his mile in a brisk 3 minutes and 43.13 seconds. When it comes to fastest women, the gold medal goes to Svetlana Masterkova of Switzerland, who completed her mile in 4 minutes and 12.56 seconds.

HEALTHY HUMANS!

One last thing: how to keep that body of yours fit and strong!

What should I eat to keep healthy?

WHAT WE NEED	WHERE WE FIND IT	HOW IT HELPS US
Carbohydrates	Rice, whole grains, and beans	Good for energy
Proteins	Fish, chicken, and eggs	Builds and supports the body
Vitamins and minerals	Fruit and vegetables	Good for our cells and organs
Fiber	Nuts, grains, fruits, and seeds	Helps to keep our digestive system running
Good fats	Olive oil, avocados, some nuts, and oily fish	Helps us absorb vitamins, create energy, and lower cholesterol

Do some foods help me build strong bones?
Sure! Calcium is the chemical that gives your skeleton a helping hand! You can find it in milk, cheese, soybeans, nuts, and some leafy vegetables. So eat your greens!

FACT OR FICTION?

Is it true that carrots give us super-vision?
Kind of! Carrots are rich in vitamin A, which your body needs to make rhodopsin. This is a pigment in your eyes that lets you see when there's not a lot of light. So eating carrots can help you produce the stuff that lets you see in the dark, but they won't let you see in total darkness.

Why should we drink water?
We should drink around 8 glasses of fluid each day. Our bodies are 75 percent water, so we need to keep it topped up to replace the fluid we lose when sweating, breathing, or peeing. Water flushes out the waste from our organs, carries nutrients to cells, and helps us manage our body temperature.

Why should we keep fit?
Being active helps us build a stronger heart, bones, and muscles. It encourages our growth, improves our balance, and even gives us a better night's sleep. Exercise can help improve our grades, too! Regular activity improves concentration, thinking, and remembering all the facts in this book!

CHECK OUT ALL OF THE FANTASTIC FACTS IN THIS SENSATIONAL SERIES!